The Clue Books

FLOWERS

GWEN ALLEN
JOAN DENSLOW

illustrations by
ROSEMARY LEE
TIM HALLIDAY

OXFORD
UNIVERSITY
PRESS

2

Oxford University Press, Walton Street, Oxford OX2 6DP

OXFORD NEW YORK TORONTO
DELHI BOMBAY CALCUTTA MADRAS KARACHI
PETALING JAYA SINGAPORE HONG KONG TOKYO
NAIROBI DAR ES SALAAM CAPE TOWN
MELBOURNE AUCKLAND
and associated companies in
BERLIN IBADAN

Oxford is a trade mark of Oxford University Press

First published 1969
Reprinted 1971 with corrections, 1974, 1976,
1978, 1980, 1983, 1985, 1989, 1991

PRINTED IN HONG KONG

Some spring and summer flowers

I   2   3   4   5   6   7   8

Flowers have many different shapes and colours. If you look at them through a magnifying lens, you will see even more shapes.

Botanists study the shapes and arrangements of flowers and leaves, and put flowers that are alike into groups called families.

By collecting flowers and studying pages 4–18 you will be able to recognise these different shapes and arrangements. Then when you use the clues on pages 20–26 you will find first the family and then the name of the flower.

Collect flowers from waste land and the roadside, from woods, fields, heaths, mountains, valleys, river banks, and by the sea at different times of the year.

The lines on this page represent the heights of plants drawn.

1 cm. on the line represents 12 cms. on the real plant.

Using this scale find out the height of each plant in the picture opposite.

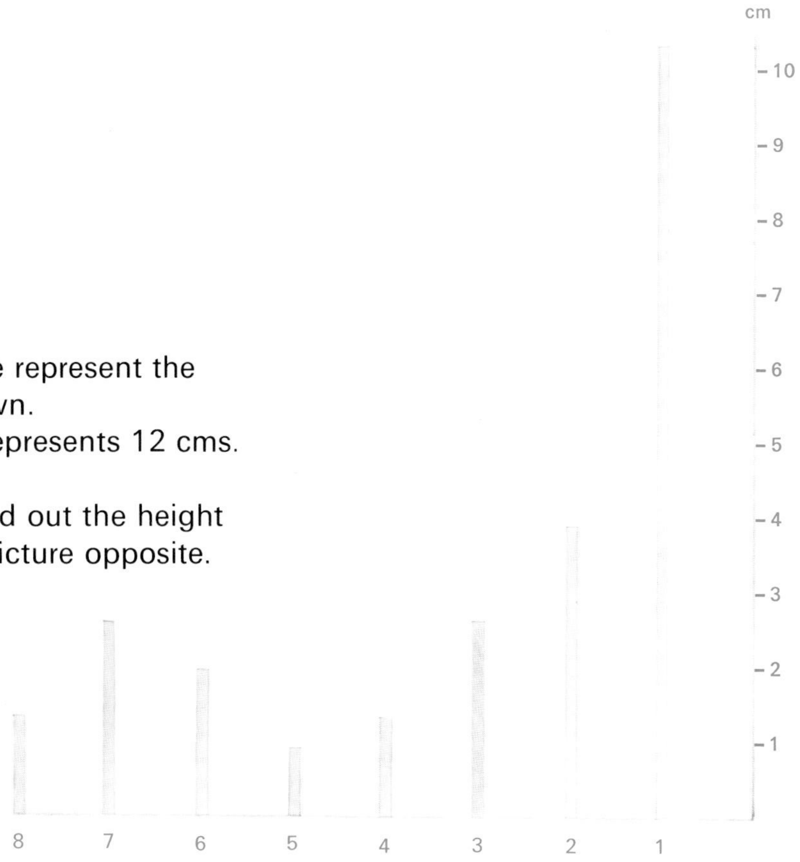

cm

— 10

— 9

— 8

— 7

— 6

— 5

— 4

— 3

— 2

— 1

8   7   6   5   4   3   2   1

FLOWERS

Most flowers have *petals*, which are usually the most brightly coloured part.
The petals of a flower are not always all the same shape.

The petals may be all the same shape and size, (1–3).

or   The petals may be of different shapes and sizes, (4–6).

or   Each petal-like part may be a complete small flower
called a *floret*, (7–8).

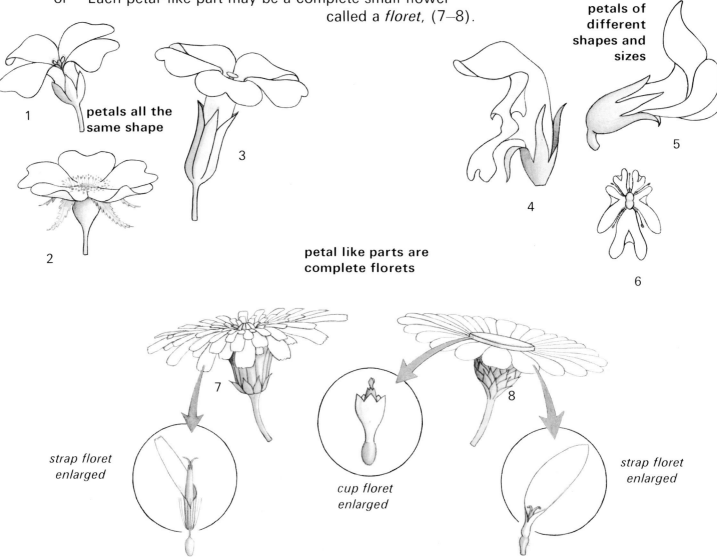

petals all the
same shape

petals of
different
shapes and
sizes

1

2

3

4

5

6

petal like parts are
complete florets

7

8

*strap floret
enlarged*

*cup floret
enlarged*

*strap floret
enlarged*

Collect as many flowers as you can and then find out to which group each belongs. There are many more in each group than have been illustrated.

Keep the flowers belonging to the same groups together and press them.

HOW TO PRESS FLOWERS

Find two pieces of stiff cardboard or hardboard, about 20 × 30 cm, and some sheets of newspaper about the same size. Put one of the pieces of board flat on the floor or on a table and cover it with two or three sheets of newspaper. Now carefully spread out some of the flowers you have collected on the top sheet of newspaper. Cover them with two or three more sheets of newspaper. If you have more flowers, make another layer. When you have put in all the flowers you want to press, cover the top layer with some more newspaper and the other piece of board. Put some heavy books on top to weigh it down.

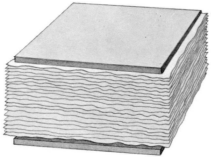

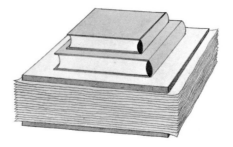

ter a few days carefully take the flowers from between the
ers of newspaper. Stick them into a book with blank pages,
ping a separate page for each petal shape.

*The pages of your book
will look like this*

6   Most flowers with petals have small green *sepals* outside the petals.
    These protected the flower when it was in bud.

    When sepals and petals are the same colour they are together called the *perianth*.

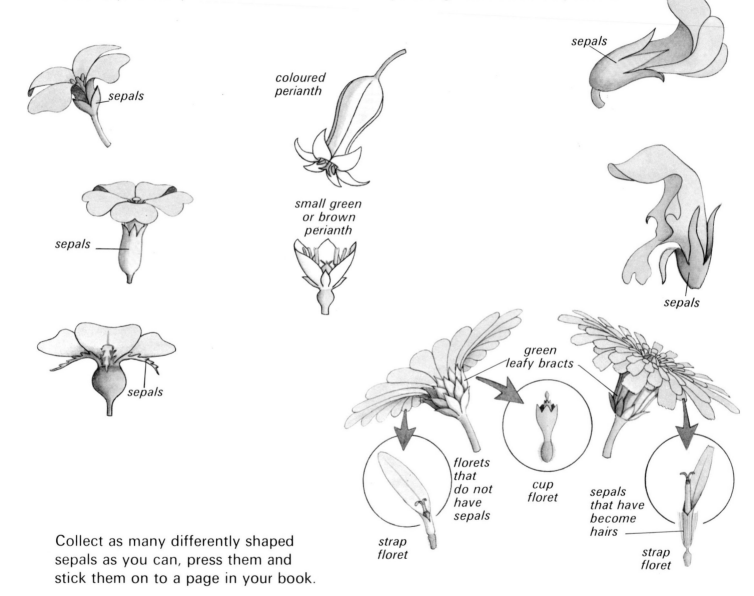

Collect as many differently shaped
sepals as you can, press them and
stick them on to a page in your book.

Inside the flower, next to the petals and sometimes attached to them, are the *stamens* which produce the pollen.

When the stamens are ripe they burst to scatter the pollen.

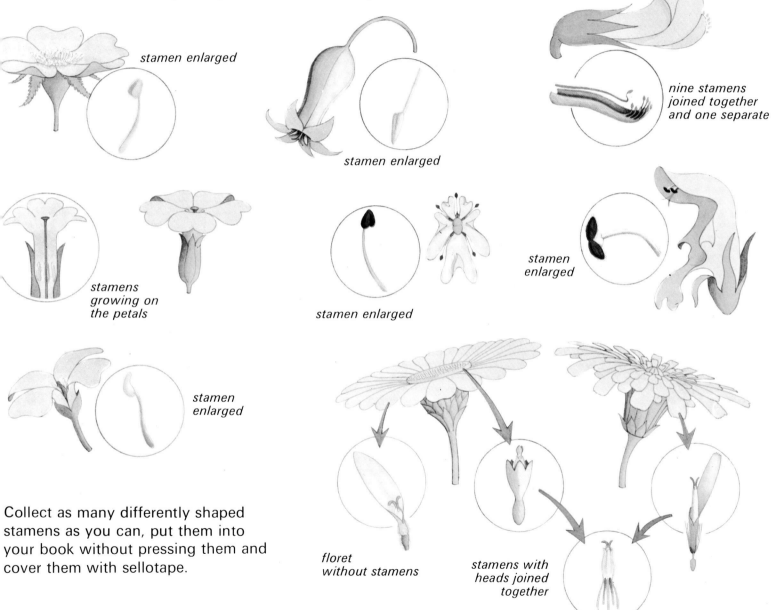

stamen enlarged

stamen enlarged

nine stamens joined together and one separate

stamens growing on the petals

stamen enlarged

stamen enlarged

stamen enlarged

Collect as many differently shaped stamens as you can, put them into your book without pressing them and cover them with sellotape.

floret without stamens

stamens with heads joined together

8   In the middle of the flower is the part called the *pistil*.

At the bottom of the pistil is the part that grows into the fruit and which contains the seeds.

This is called the *ovary*.

On top of the ovary is the *stigma* which catches the pollen scattered by the stamens. Most seeds will grow only if pollen is caught by the stigma.
Sometimes insects carry the pollen. Sometimes the wind blows it.

Look at flowers through a magnifying lens, peel back the petals and sepals so that you can see the pistil more clearly.

It is easier to see the shape of the ovary in an older flower.

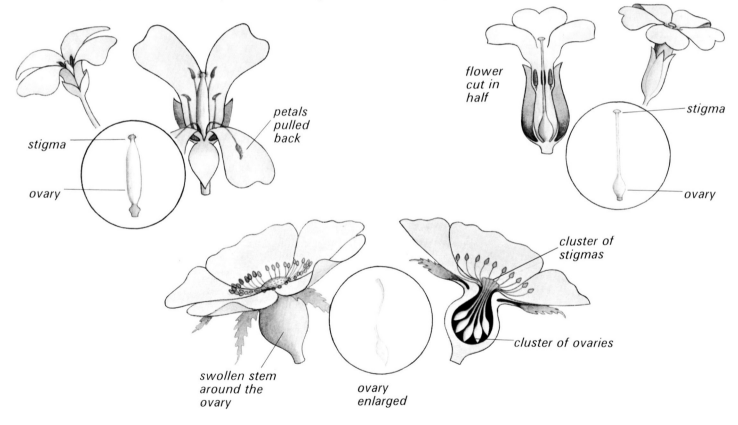

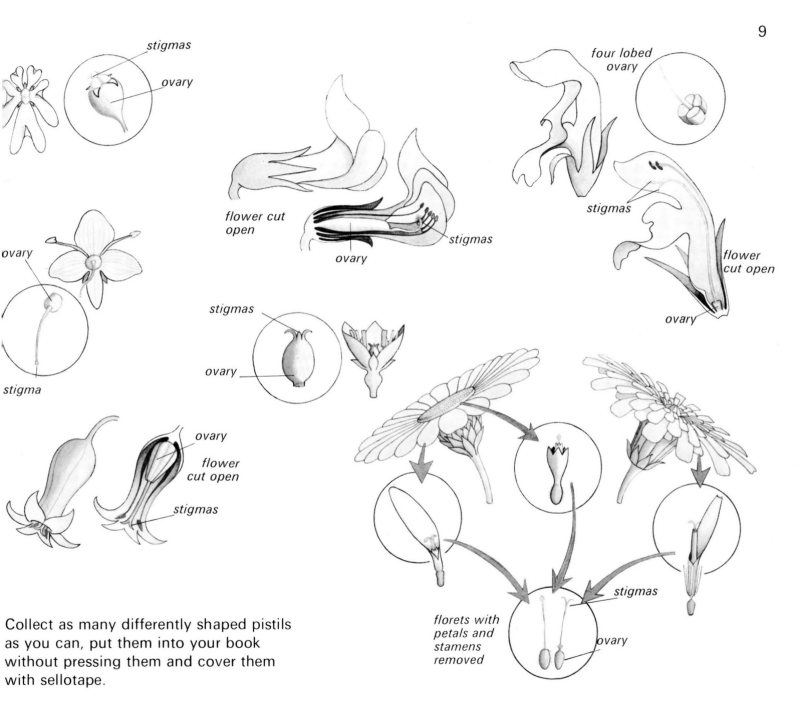

stigmas

ovary

four lobed ovary

stigmas

flower cut open

ovary

ovary

stigma

flower cut open

ovary

stigmas

stigmas

ovary

ovary

flower cut open

stigmas

stigmas

ovary

florets with petals and stamens removed

Collect as many differently shaped pistils as you can, put them into your book without pressing them and cover them with sellotape.

10   Some flowers do not have petals or sepals, but because they have either stamens or a pistil or both they are still called flowers.

Most grasses have stamens and a pistil in the same flower, protected by leafy bracts.

Sedges usually have separate clusters of flowers, some with stamens and some with a pistil.

Many trees have two kinds of flower: clusters of flowers with stamens forming catkins, and flowers with a pistil which are smaller and less easy to see.

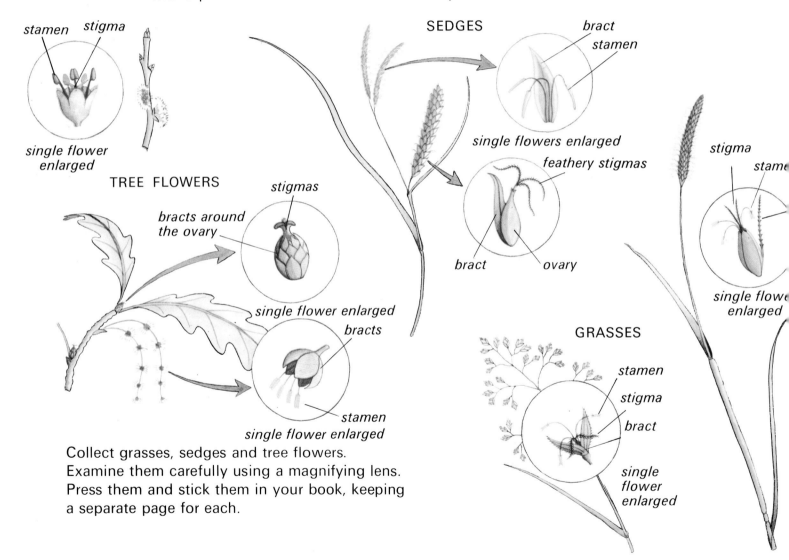

stamen   stigma

single flower enlarged

TREE FLOWERS

SEDGES

bract
stamen

single flowers enlarged

stigmas

bracts around the ovary

feathery stigmas

single flower enlarged

bract   ovary

bracts

stamen

single flower enlarged

stigma

stamen

single flower enlarged

GRASSES

stamen

stigma

bract

single flower enlarged

Collect grasses, sedges and tree flowers.
Examine them carefully using a magnifying lens.
Press them and stick them in your book, keeping
a separate page for each.

FRUITS

The ovary of the flower becomes the fruit containing the seeds.

The illustrations show how the fruit grows in two different flowers. In one the fruit grows inside the flower; in the other it grows below the petals.

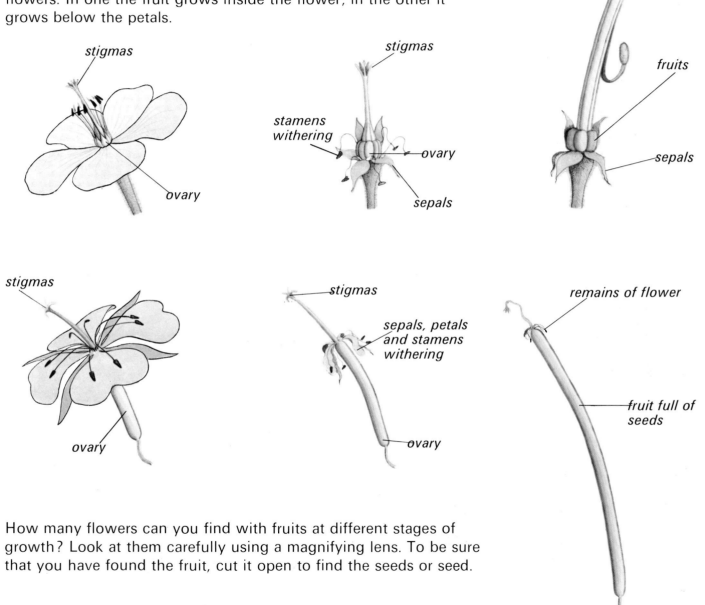

How many flowers can you find with fruits at different stages of growth? Look at them carefully using a magnifying lens. To be sure that you have found the fruit, cut it open to find the seeds or seed.

You will have noticed that fruits vary in shape and that the seeds are arranged in different ways inside them.

The seeds will grow into new plants: they may be scattered on to new ground from the plant or collected by gardeners and farmers.

Fruits may be either:

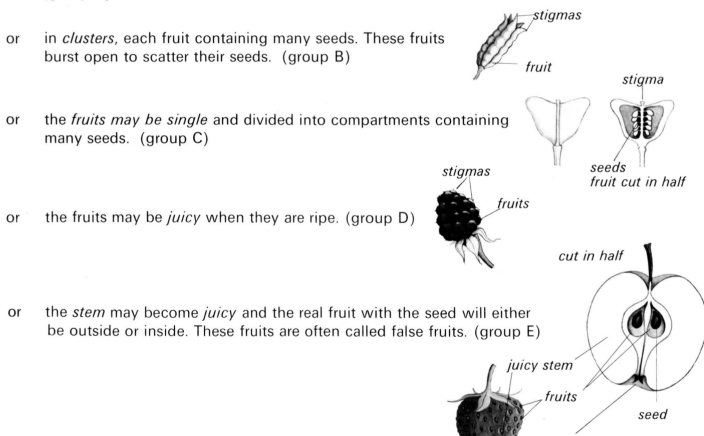

arranged in clusters, each fruit containing one seed. The single fruits are scattered with the seed inside them, these fruits do not burst open. (group A)

or   in *clusters*, each fruit containing many seeds. These fruits burst open to scatter their seeds. (group B)

or   the *fruits may be single* and divided into compartments containing many seeds. (group C)

or   the fruits may be *juicy* when they are ripe. (group D)

or   the *stem* may become *juicy* and the real fruit with the seed will either be outside or inside. These fruits are often called false fruits. (group E)

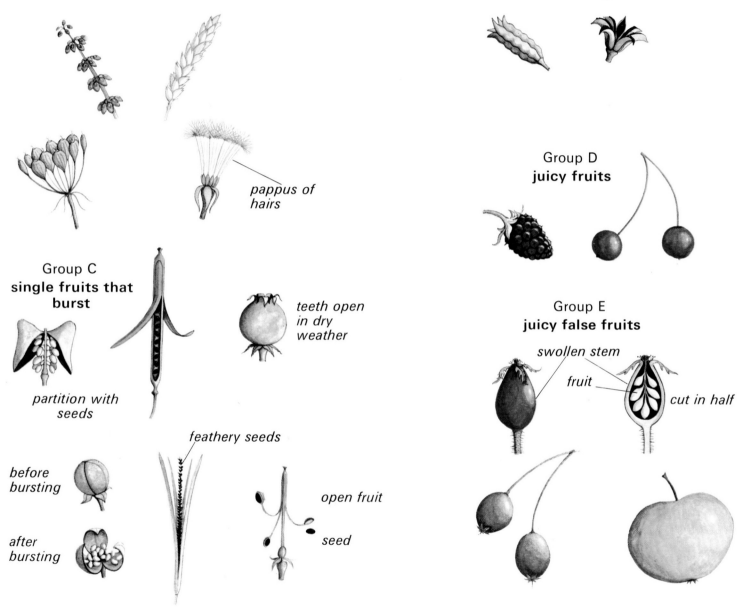

Group A
clusters of fruits that do not burst

pappus of hairs

Group C
single fruits that burst

partition with seeds

teeth open in dry weather

feathery seeds

before bursting

after bursting

open fruit

seed

Group B
clusters of bursting fruits

Group D
juicy fruits

Group E
juicy false fruits

swollen stem

fruit

cut in half

Collect as many different flowers as you can, with stems as long as possible. You will see that the flowers are arranged on the stem in different ways.

They may grow *singly*

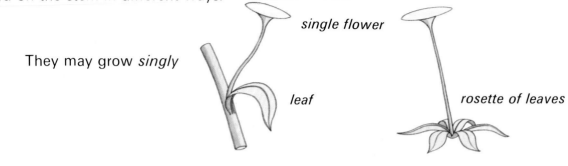

single flower

leaf

rosette of leaves

or be arranged in *groups* on the stem.
The groups may be arranged in

Spikes, when the flowers have no stalks and the oldest flower is at the bottom of the stem.

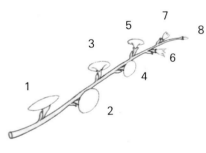

or   *Racemes,* when the flowers have stalks and the oldest is at the bottom of the stem.

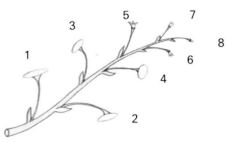

or
a *Corymb,* when the flower stalks grow from different levels on the stem but the flowers are almost at the same level, the oldest flower growing from the bottom of the stem.

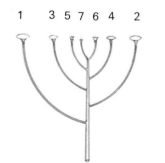

or   a *Capitulum,* when many florets are in one head on a flattened stem, surrounded by green bracts.

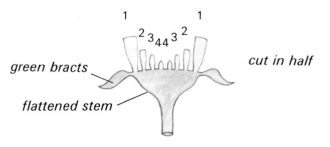

green bracts

flattened stem

cut in half

or   an *Umbel,* when the flower stalks grow from the same point on the stem.

or   an *Umbel of Umbels,* when a number of umbels grow from the same point on the stem.

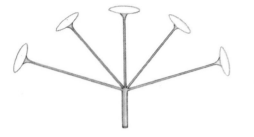

or   a *Cyme,* when each main stalk ends in a flower and younger flowers grow out from the stem below this.

The *Cyme* may be one-sided, when the flowers all grow out from the same side of the stem.

or   the *Cyme* may be two-sided when the flowers grow out from both sides of the stem.

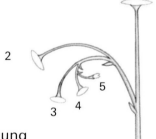

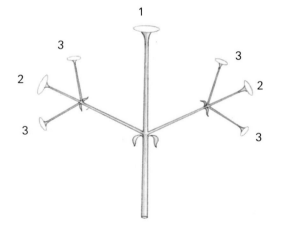

When the plant is young the one-sided cyme is coiled like a spring.

How are the flowers you have collected arranged on their stems? Find as many other arrangements as you can, press them and stick them into your book keeping a separate page for each group.

When you are studying flowers and wish to name them you will need to know about the leaves and the way they are arranged on the stem.

Make a collection of leaves of different shapes.

They may be *simple* because they have only one part.

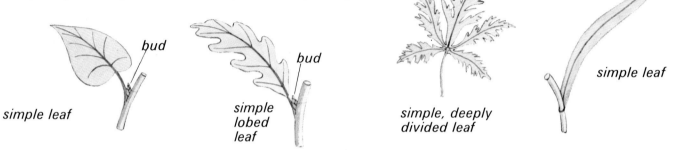

bud

bud

simple leaf

simple leaf

simple lobed leaf

simple, deeply divided leaf

or   *compound* because they have several separate parts called leaflets. A bud is often seen at the base of the leaf stalk. The bud may have grown into a leafy stem or a flower or may not yet be visible. There are no buds where the leaflets join the leaf stalk.

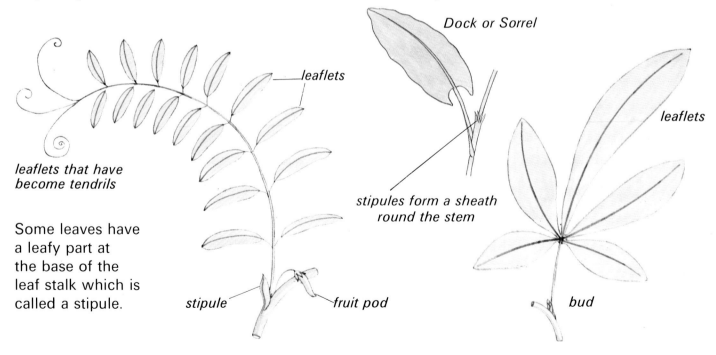

leaflets that have become tendrils

Some leaves have a leafy part at the base of the leaf stalk which is called a stipule.

stipule

fruit pod

leaflets

Dock or Sorrel

stipules form a sheath round the stem

leaflets

bud

When you have a good collection of leaves of different shapes, press them (page 5) and put them in your book keeping a page for each group.

Another way of recording leaf shapes is by making scribble prints.

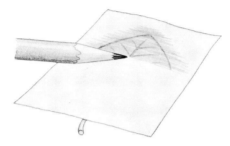

To make these you will need some plain paper, wax crayons or coloured pencils with thick centres.

Place the leaf underside upwards on a flat surface.
Cover it with a piece of plain paper a little larger than the leaf.

Scribble gently over the leaf with the crayon until its shape and markings show clearly.

Cut the paper to the shape of the leaf, about half an inch away from it all the way round.

Make a collection of scribble prints in your book arranging them according to their shapes.

The markings on the leaves are veins.
They may be arranged in a *network*   or   be *parallel*.

Collect a number of net-veined and parallel-veined leaves, press them or make scribble prints of them and put them in your book.

Leaves may be arranged on the stem in different ways.

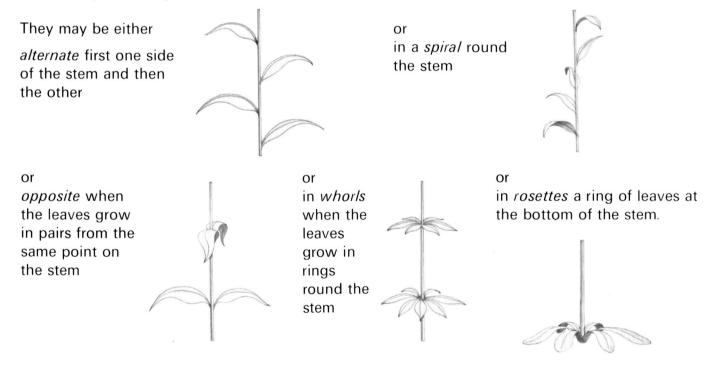

They may be either

alternate first one side of the stem and then the other

or
in a *spiral* round the stem

or
opposite when the leaves grow in pairs from the same point on the stem

or
in *whorls* when the leaves grow in rings round the stem

or
in *rosettes* a ring of leaves at the bottom of the stem.

Look for small plants with these arrangements so that you can press them, and put them in your book keeping a page for each group.

Now that you have looked at the different parts of a flower, read page 3 again.

When you collect flowers for naming remember you also need to know about leaves. If the plant is common (there are many of them) pick as much of the plant as possible, including the fruits. If it is rare (less than 12 plants) do *not* pick it; make drawings of its parts and write about the flowers and leaves in a book which you will need to carry with you when you are collecting plants. This sort of book is called a Field Notebook.

When you have picked a flower, use the following clues to find out what its name is and to which family it belongs. Then you can press it and stick it in your book and write the name underneath it.

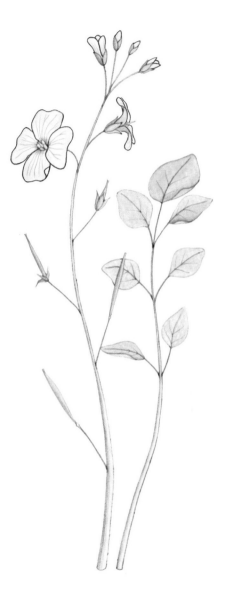

20 Look carefully at your plant, find the clue that fits it, then you will know where to go for the next clue.

CLUES TO COMMON FLOWER FAMILIES

| Clue 1 | If the plant has woody stems it is a tree or shrub; | go to clue 31. |
| | If the stems of the plant are *not* woody | go to clue 2. |

Clue 2	If the flower has both petals and sepals (pages 4 and 6)	go to clue 3.
	If each petal-like part is a complete flower called a floret (pages 4 and 14)	go to clue 18.
	If the petals and sepals form a perianth (page 6)	go to clue 19.
	If the flower has *no* petals, sepals or perianth	go to clue 29.

| Clue 3 | If the flower has petals of the same shape and size (page 4) | go to clue 4. |
| | If the flower has petals of different shapes and sizes | go to clue 13. |

| Clue 4 | If the petals are joined together | go to clue 10. |
| | If the petals are *not* joined together | go to clue 5. |

one petal

| Clue 5 | If the flower has 4 petals | go to clue 6. |
| | If the flower has 5 petals (sometimes more) | go to clue 7. |

| Clue 6 | If the flower has 6 stamens, 4 long and 2 short and the ovary is inside the petals it belongs to the WALLFLOWER FAMILY; | turn to pages 30, 31. |

If the flower has 4 stamens and the ovary is below the petals it belongs to the WILLOWHERB FAMILY; turn to page 34.

If the flower has many stamens and the stem has a milky or coloured juice it belongs to the POPPY FAMILY; turn to page 29.

If the flower has many stamens and the stem does not have a milky or coloured juice it belongs to the ROSE FAMILY; turn to pages 38, 39.

Clue 7

If the flower has many stamens, joined together and leaves in opposite pairs (see page 18) it belongs to the ST. JOHN'S WORT FAMILY; turn to page 33.

If the flower has many stamens joined together and leaves in a spiral it belongs to the MALLOW FAMILY; turn to page 35.

If the flower has more than 10 separate stamens — go to clue 8.

If the flower has 5 stamens or 10 stamens — go to clue 9.

Clue 8

If the flower has one or more ovaries below the petals (page 11) often inside a swollen stem (page 12) and leaves with stipules (page 16) it belongs to the ROSE FAMILY; turn to pages 38, 39.

If the flower has one or more ovaries not below the petals, and the leaves have leaflets and stipules it belongs to the ROSE FAMILY; turn to pages 38, 39.

If the flower has clusters of ovaries (page 12) and the leaves do not have stipules it belongs to the BUTTERCUP FAMILY; turn to pages 28, 29

Clue 9

If the flowers are arranged in a two sided cyme (page 15) it belongs to the PINK FAMILY; turn to pages 32, 33.

If the flowers are solitary or a few together and the fruit separates into parts like this; it belongs to the GERANIUM FAMILY; turn to page 35.

stigmas

fruit

Clue 10	If the petal tube separates at the top into 5 parts	go to clue 11.
	If the petal tube separates at the top into 4 parts and the plant has leaves in whorls (page 18) it belongs to the BEDSTRAW FAMILY;	turn to page 54.
Clue 11	If the ovary grows inside the flower (page 11) and the stamens are attached to the petals (page 7)	go to clue 12.

stamens still attached to petals

sepal tube

petal tube

	If the ovary grows below the petals (page 11) and the stamens are not attached to the petals it belongs to the BELLFLOWER FAMILY;	turn to page 54.
Clue 12	If the flowers are arranged in a one-sided cyme (page 15) it belongs to the BORAGE FAMILY or NIGHTSHADE FAMILY	turn to page 45.
	If the flowers grow singly, or are arranged in umbels or racemes (pages 14 and 15) it belongs to the PRIMROSE FAMILY;	turn to page 44.
Clue 13	If the petals are flat and only slightly different in shape	go to clue 14.
	If the petals are very different in shape and size	go to clue 16.
Clue 14	If the flowers are arranged in umbels of umbels (page 15) it belongs to the PARSLEY FAMILY;	turn to pages 40, 41.
	If the flowers are *not* arranged in this way	go to clue 15.

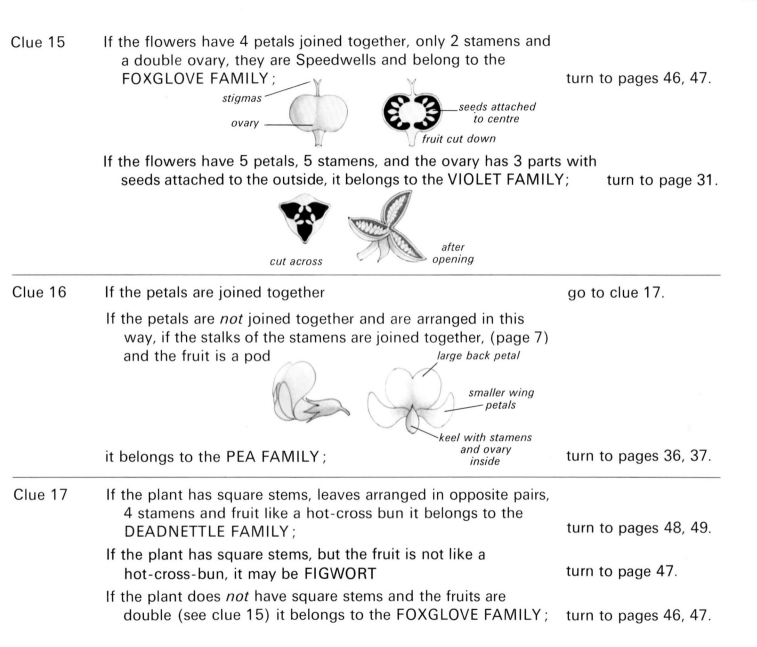

Clue 15   If the flowers have 4 petals joined together, only 2 stamens and
a double ovary, they are Speedwells and belong to the
FOXGLOVE FAMILY;   turn to pages 46, 47.

stigmas

ovary

seeds attached
to centre

fruit cut down

If the flowers have 5 petals, 5 stamens, and the ovary has 3 parts with
seeds attached to the outside, it belongs to the VIOLET FAMILY;   turn to page 31.

cut across

after
opening

Clue 16   If the petals are joined together   go to clue 17.

If the petals are *not* joined together and are arranged in this
way, if the stalks of the stamens are joined together, (page 7)
and the fruit is a pod

large back petal

smaller wing
petals

keel with stamens
and ovary
inside

it belongs to the PEA FAMILY;   turn to pages 36, 37.

Clue 17   If the plant has square stems, leaves arranged in opposite pairs,
4 stamens and fruit like a hot-cross bun it belongs to the
DEADNETTLE FAMILY;   turn to pages 48, 49.

If the plant has square stems, but the fruit is not like a
hot-cross-bun, it may be FIGWORT   turn to page 47.

If the plant does *not* have square stems and the fruits are
double (see clue 15) it belongs to the FOXGLOVE FAMILY;   turn to pages 46, 47.

24

Clue 18	If each floret has 4 separate stamens and a single stigma it belongs to the SCABIOUS FAMILY;	turn to page 54.
from clue 2	If each floret has 5 stamens joined at the top and a stigma that divides into 2 parts it belongs to the DAISY FAMILY;	turn to pages 50–53.
Clue 19	If the perianth is small, green or brown or pinkish	go to clue 20.
from clue 2	If the perianth is large and petal-like	go to clue 25.
Clue 20	If the leaves have net veins (page 18)	go to clue 21.
	If the leaves have parallel veins it belongs to the RUSH FAMILY;	turn to page 57.
Clue 21	If the leaves grow in a rosette (page 18) and the flower stalk has no leaves it belongs to the PLANTAIN FAMILY;	turn to page 43.
	If the stems are leafy, with many clusters of flowers usually in spikes and racemes (page 14)	go to clue 22.
Clue 22	If the flowers look like this it belongs to the SPURGE FAMILY;	turn to page 41.
	If the flowers have either stamens or ovary, but not both it may be DOG'S MERCURY (Spurge family);	turn to page 41.
	If the flowers are *not* like this	go to clue 23.
Clue 23	If the leaves have stipules (page 16) forming a sheath round the stem it belongs to the DOCK FAMILY;	turn to page 42.
	If the leaves do not have stipules	go to clue 24.

stamens, ovary, stigmas

Clue 24	If the leaves have stinging hairs it belongs to the NETTLE FAMILY;	turn to page 43.
	If the leaves do not have stinging hairs it belongs to the GOOSEFOOT FAMILY;	turn to page 43.

Clue 25   If the perianth parts are very different in shape and size, it belongs to the ORCHID FAMILY;   turn to page 58.

two clusters of pollen — perianth — spur — ovary

If the perianth is not like this   go to clue 26.

Clue 26	If the ovary is inside the perianth (page 11)	go to clue 27.
	If the ovary is below the perianth	go to clue 28.

Clue 27	If the ovary is a cluster of separate parts (page 12) and the leaves have net veins it belongs to the BUTTERCUP FAMILY;	turn to pages 28, 29.
	If the ovary is a cluster of separate parts and the leaves have parallel veins it belongs to the WATER PLANTAIN FAMILY;	turn to page 55.
	If the ovary is single with 3 divisions it belongs to the LILY FAMILY;	turn to page 56.

Clue 28	If the flower has 3 stamens it belongs to the IRIS FAMILY;	turn to page 58.
	If the flower has 6 stamens it belongs to the SNOWDROP FAMILY;	turn to page 56.

| Clue 29 | If the plant has leaves that float on, or grow under the water it belongs to the PONDWEED FAMILY; | turn to page 55. |
| from clue 2 | If the plant does not grow in water and has grass-like leaves with parallel veins | go to clue 30. |

| Clue 30 | If the stem is hollow and there is a leafy ligule where the leaf sheath begins it belongs to the GRASS FAMILY; | turn to pages 60, 61. |

ligule

leaf sheath
around the stem

| | If the stem is solid and 3-sided, with no ligule where the sheath begins, it belongs to the SEDGE FAMILY; | turn to page 59. |

| Clue 31 | If the fruit is a cone and the leaves are small and needle-like it belongs to the CONIFER FAMILY; | turn to page 62. |
| from clue 1 | If the fruit is not a cone and the leaves are net-veined | go to clue 32. |

| Clue 32 | If the flowers with stamens are arranged in catkins it belongs to the CATKIN FAMILY; | turn to page 62. |
| | If the flowers are not arranged in catkins | go to clue 33. |

Clue 33	If the flowers are like those of the *pea family* (clue 16)	turn to pages 36, 37.
	If the flowers are like those of the *rose family* (clue 8)	turn to pages 38, 39.
	If the flowers are like those of the *buttercup family* and the plant climbs it is Clematis (clue 8)	turn to page 29.
	If the flowers are not like these	turn to page 62.

FLOWER FAMILIES

The places where the plants may be found, the months during which they flower and the size of the full grown plant are given below each illustration.

BUTTERCUP FAMILY
Ranunculaceae

1. Lesser Celandine
fields, waste places
Mar.– May
5–25 cm.

2. Bulbous Buttercup
meadows, waste places
May–June
15–40 cm.

3. Creeping Buttercup
fields, gardens, waste places
May–Aug.
15–60 cm.

4. Water Crowfoot
ponds, streams
June–Aug.
15–100 cm.

5. Field Buttercup
meadows, waste places
June–Aug.
15–100 cm.

6. Lesser Spearwort
marshes *June–Sept.*
8–50 cm.

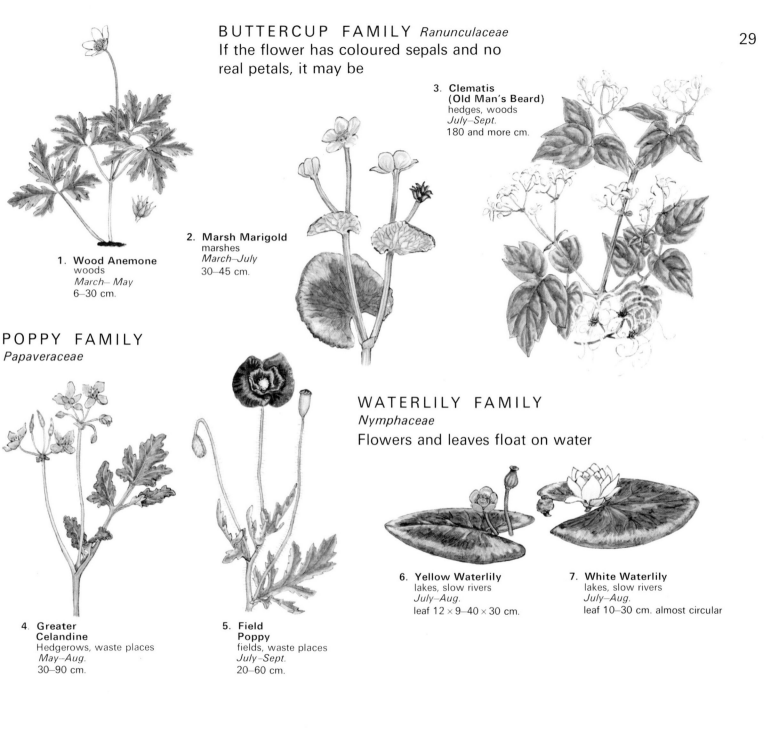

BUTTERCUP FAMILY *Ranunculaceae*
If the flower has coloured sepals and no real petals, it may be

1. Wood Anemone
woods
March– May
6–30 cm.

2. Marsh Marigold
marshes
March–July
30–45 cm.

**3. Clematis
(Old Man's Beard)**
hedges, woods
July–Sept.
180 and more cm.

POPPY FAMILY
Papaveraceae

**4. Greater
Celandine**
Hedgerows, waste places
May–Aug.
30–90 cm.

**5. Field
Poppy**
fields, waste places
July–Sept.
20–60 cm.

WATERLILY FAMILY
Nymphaceae
Flowers and leaves float on water

6. Yellow Waterlily
lakes, slow rivers
July–Aug.
leaf 12 × 9–40 × 30 cm.

7. White Waterlily
lakes, slow rivers
July–Aug.
leaf 10–30 cm. almost circular

WALLFLOWER FAMILY *Cruciferae*
If the fruits are much longer than they are wide, it may be

1. Wallflower
cliffs
April–June
20–60 cm.

2. Watercress
shallow water
April–Oct.
10–60 cm.

3. Cuckoo Flower
damp meadows
April–June
30–60 cm.

4. Field Cabbage
fields, waste places
May–Aug.
30–60 cm.

5. Garlic Mustard
(smells of onion)
hedges
April–June
20–120 cm.

6. Hedge Mustard
roadsides, waste places
June–July
30–90 cm.

7. Charlock
fields, waste places
June–Aug.
30–80 cm.

WALLFLOWER FAMILY
Cruciferae

If the fruits are about as
wide as they are long,
it may be

1. **Shepherds Purse**
   fields, gardens, waste places
   Jan.–Dec.
   3–40 cm.

2. **Pennycress**
   fields, waste
   places
   May–July
   15–30 cm.

VIOLET FAMILY
Violaceae

3. **Heartsease**
   cultivated and waste ground
   April–Sept.
   3–45 cm.

4. **Sweet Violet**
   banks, woods
   Feb.–April
   6–12 cm.

5. **Dog Violet**
   woods, banks, heaths
   April–June
   2–20 cm.

**PINK
FAMILY**
Caryophyllaceae

If the sepals are
joined together,
it may be

1. Bladder Campion
fields, waste places,
often near the sea
(Sea Campion)
June–Aug.
25–90 cm.

2. White Campion
hedges, fields, waste places
May–Sept.
30–100 cm.

3. Red Campion
woods, hedgerows
May–June
20–90 cm.

If the sepals
are not joined
together, it
may be

4. Ragged Robin
wet meadows, ditches
May–June
15–75 cm.

**5. Mouse-eared
Chickweed**
woods, fields,
waste places
April–Sept.
15–45 cm.

6. Greater Stitchwort
hedgerows, woods
May–June
15–60 cm.

PINK FAMILY
Caryophyllaceae

If the sepals are not joined together and the plant is trailing, it may be

MIGNONETTE FAMILY
Resedaceae

1. Chickweed
fields, gardens, waste places
Jan.–Dec.
5–40 cm.

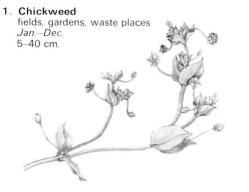

2. Pearlwort
waste and stony places
April–Aug.
3–18 cm.

3. Wild Mignonette
waste places
June–Aug.
30–75 cm.

ST. JOHN'S WORT FAMILY
Hypericaceae

FLAX FAMILY
Linaceae

**4. Common
St. John's Wort**
woods, hedgerows
June–Sept.
30–90 cm.

**5. Slender
St. John's Wort**
dry woods, open
heaths
June–Aug.
30–60 cm.

6. Fairy Flax
meadows, pastures
June–Aug.
5–25 cm.

WILLOWHERB FAMILY
Onagraceae

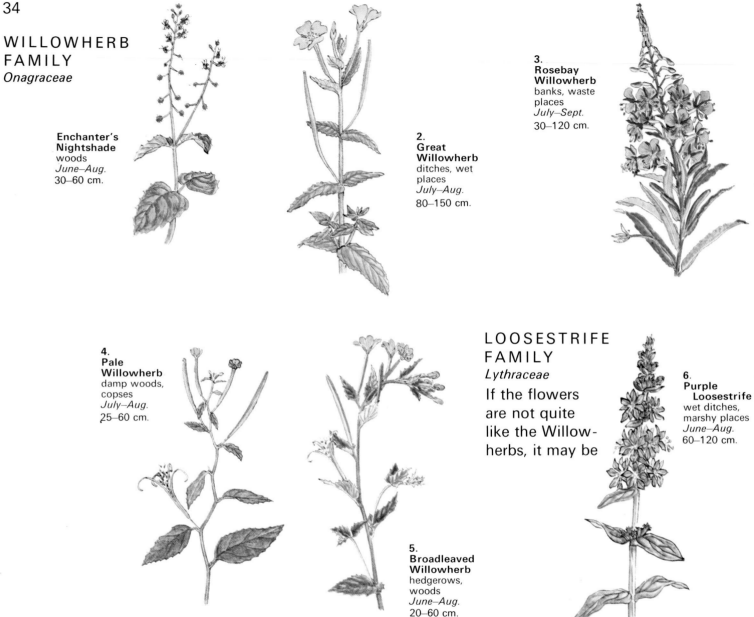

Enchanter's Nightshade
woods
June–Aug.
30–60 cm.

**2.
Great Willowherb**
ditches, wet places
July–Aug.
80–150 cm.

**3.
Rosebay Willowherb**
banks, waste places
July–Sept.
30–120 cm.

**4.
Pale Willowherb**
damp woods, copses
July–Aug.
25–60 cm.

**5.
Broadleaved Willowherb**
hedgerows, woods
June–Aug.
20–60 cm.

LOOSESTRIFE FAMILY
Lythraceae

If the flowers are not quite like the Willowherbs, it may be

**6.
Purple Loosestrife**
wet ditches, marshy places
June–Aug.
60–120 cm.

1. **Dovesfoot Cranesbill**
waste and cultivated places
April–Sept.
10–40 cm.

2. **Cut leaved Cranesbill**
dry pastures, waste places
April–Aug.
10–60 cm.

3. **Herb Robert**
woods, cultivated places
May–Sept.
10–50 cm.

MALLOW FAMILY
Malvaceae

6. **Cut leaved Mallow**
hedgerows
July–Aug.
30–80 cm.

5. **Mallow**
hedgerows,
waste places
June–Sept.
45–90 cm.

4. **Meadow Cranesbill**
meadows,
hedgerows
June–Sept.
30–80 cm.

If the plant has leaves with three leaflets, it may be

1. **Spotted Medick**
waste places
April–Aug.
10–60 cm.

2. **Black Medick**
waste places,
grassland
April–Aug.
5–50 cm.

3. **Hop Trefoil**
dry meadows
June–Sept.
30–35 cm.

4. **Bird's foot Trefoil**
meadows,
grassland
June–Sept.
10–40 cm.

5. **Red Clover**
meadows,
grassland
May–June
30–60 cm.

6. **White Clover**
meadows,
grassland
June–Sept.
30–50 cm.

7. **Broom**
(woody stems)
heaths,
waste places
May–June
60–200 cm.

If the plant has many leaflets and some tendrils, it may be a Vetch

1. **Common Vetch**
   banks, waste places
   April–Sept.
   15–90 cm.

2. **Tufted Vetch**
   hedges *June–Aug.*
   60–200 cm.

3. **Bush Vetch**
   woods, hedgerows
   April–Aug.
   30–100 cm.

If the plant has prickles it is

If the plant has only 2 or 3 pairs of leaflets and tendrils, it may be

4. **Meadow Pea**
   moist meadows
   April–Aug.
   30–120 cm.

5. **Gorse**
   (woody stems)
   sandy heaths
   March–June
   60–200 cm.

ROSE FAMILY *Rosaceae*

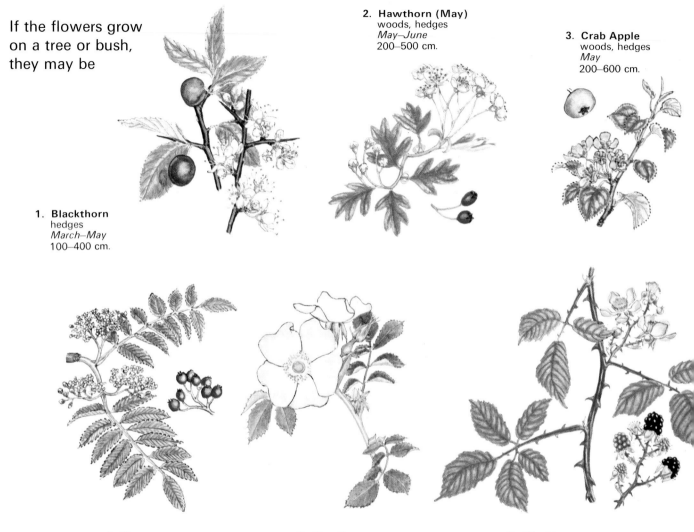

If the flowers grow
on a tree or bush,
they may be

2. Hawthorn (May)
woods, hedges
May–June
200–500 cm.

3. Crab Apple
woods, hedges
May
200–600 cm.

1. Blackthorn
hedges
March–May
100–400 cm.

**4. Rowan
(Mountain Ash)**
woods
May–June
1500–2000 cm.

5. Dog Rose
hedges
June–July
100–300 cm.

6. Blackberry
woods, hedges, waste places
June–Sept.
120 or more cm.

ROSE FAMILY *Rosaceae*
If the plant is not woody, it may be

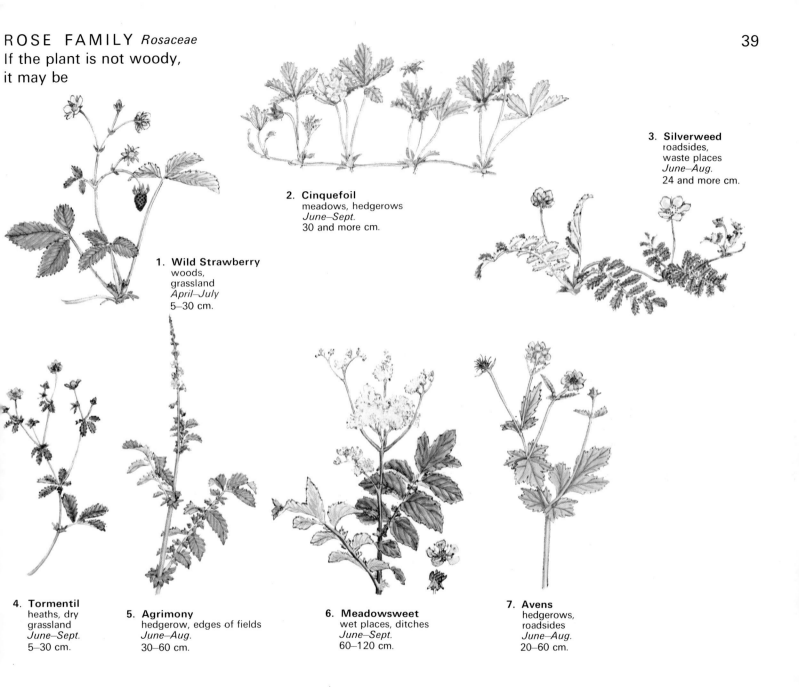

1. Wild Strawberry
woods,
grassland
April–July
5–30 cm.

2. Cinquefoil
meadows, hedgerows
June–Sept.
30 and more cm.

3. Silverweed
roadsides,
waste places
June–Aug.
24 and more cm.

4. Tormentil
heaths, dry
grassland
June–Sept.
5–30 cm.

5. Agrimony
hedgerow, edges of fields
June–Aug.
30–60 cm.

6. Meadowsweet
wet places, ditches
June–Sept.
60–120 cm.

7. Avens
hedgerows,
roadsides
June–Aug.
20–60 cm.

PARSLEY FAMILY *Umbelliferae*
If the fruits are smooth, it may be

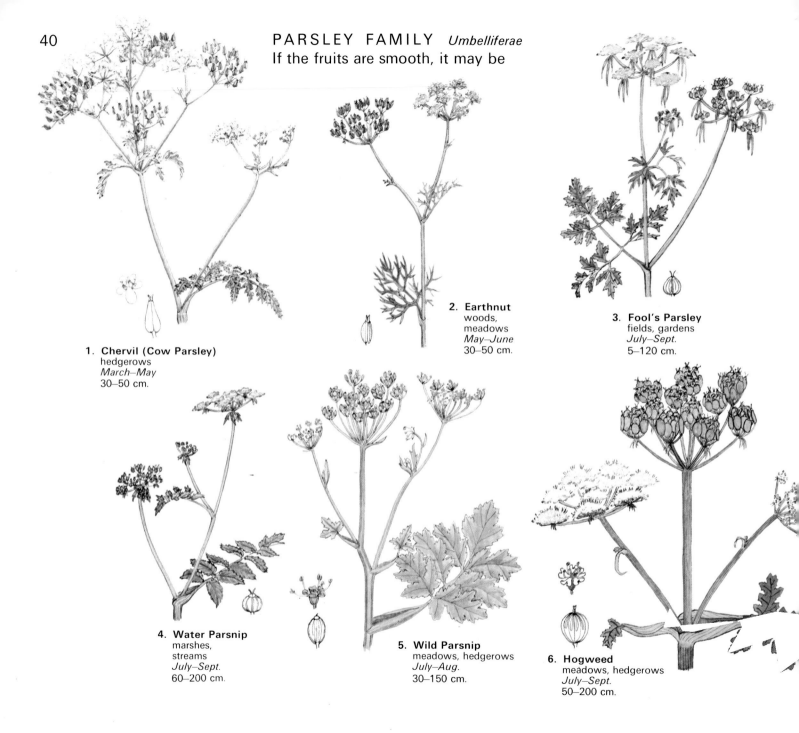

1. Chervil (Cow Parsley)
hedgerows
March–May
30–50 cm.

2. Earthnut
woods,
meadows
May–June
30–50 cm.

3. Fool's Parsley
fields, gardens
July–Sept.
5–120 cm.

4. Water Parsnip
marshes,
streams
July–Sept.
60–200 cm.

5. Wild Parsnip
meadows, hedgerows
July–Aug.
30–150 cm.

6. Hogweed
meadows, hedgerows
July–Sept.
50–200 cm.

PARSLEY FAMILY *Umbelliferae*
If the fruits are smooth, it may be

If the fruits are prickly, it may be

41

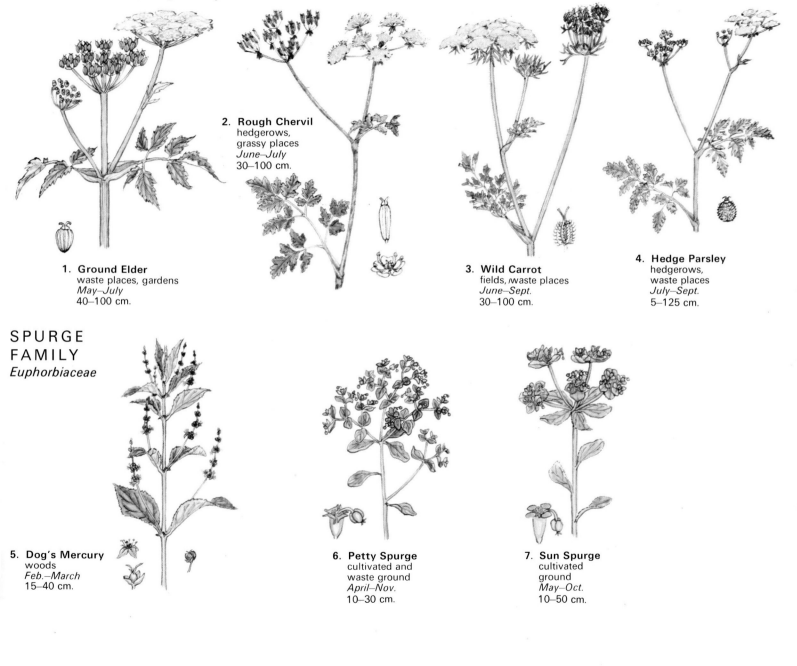

1. **Ground Elder**
waste places, gardens
May–July
40–100 cm.

2. **Rough Chervil**
hedgerows,
grassy places
June–July
30–100 cm.

3. **Wild Carrot**
fields, waste places
June–Sept.
30–100 cm.

4. **Hedge Parsley**
hedgerows,
waste places
July–Sept.
5–125 cm.

SPURGE FAMILY
Euphorbiaceae

5. **Dog's Mercury**
woods
Feb.–March
15–40 cm.

6. **Petty Spurge**
cultivated and
waste ground
April–Nov.
10–30 cm.

7. **Sun Spurge**
cultivated
ground
May–Oct.
10–50 cm.

DOCK FAMILY *Polygonaceae*
Flowers with 6 perianth parts

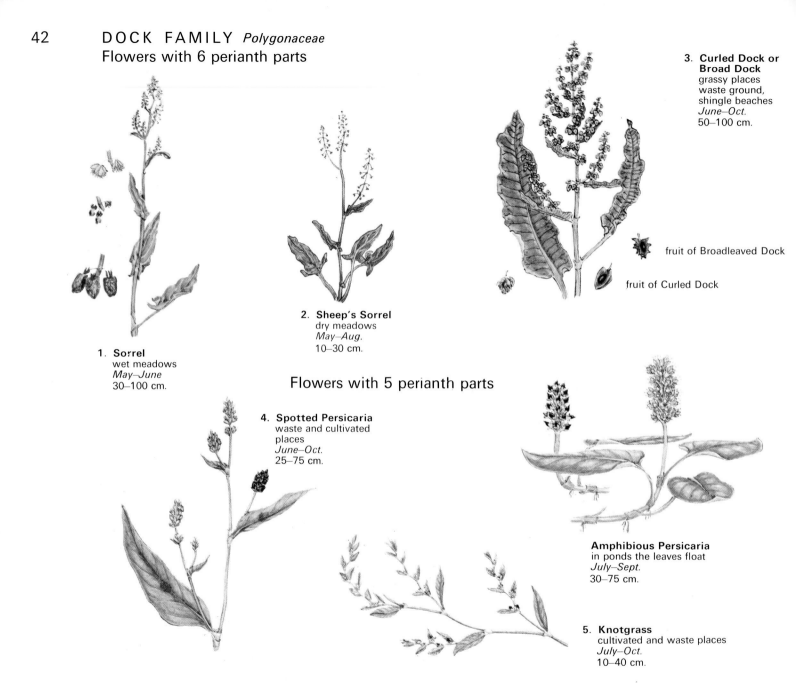

3. **Curled Dock or
   Broad Dock**
   grassy places
   waste ground,
   shingle beaches
   June–Oct.
   50–100 cm.

fruit of Broadleaved Dock

fruit of Curled Dock

2. **Sheep's Sorrel**
   dry meadows
   May–Aug.
   10–30 cm.

1. **Sorrel**
   wet meadows
   May–June
   30–100 cm.

Flowers with 5 perianth parts

4. **Spotted Persicaria**
   waste and cultivated
   places
   June–Oct.
   25–75 cm.

Amphibious Persicaria
in ponds the leaves float
July–Sept.
30–75 cm.

5. **Knotgrass**
   cultivated and waste places
   July–Oct.
   10–40 cm.

GOOSEFOOT FAMILY *Chenopodiaceae*
Stamens and ovaries in the same flower

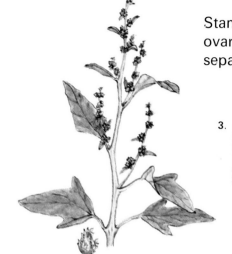

Stamens and ovaries in separate flowers

3. Common Orache
leaves powdery,
gardens, waste
places
Aug.–Oct.
30–90 cm.

1. Wild Beet
seashore *July–Sept.*
30–120 cm.

2. White Goosefoot
leaves powdery, gardens,
waste places *July–Oct.*
30–60 cm.

PLANTAIN FAMILY *Plantaginaceae*

NETTLE FAMILY *Urticaceae*

5. Greater Plantain
roadsides, grass,
cultivated land
May–Sept.
10–15 cm.

4. Ribwort
waste places,
grassland *April–Aug.*
10–15 cm.

6. Stinging Nettle
banks, woods,
near farms
June–Aug.
30–150 cm.

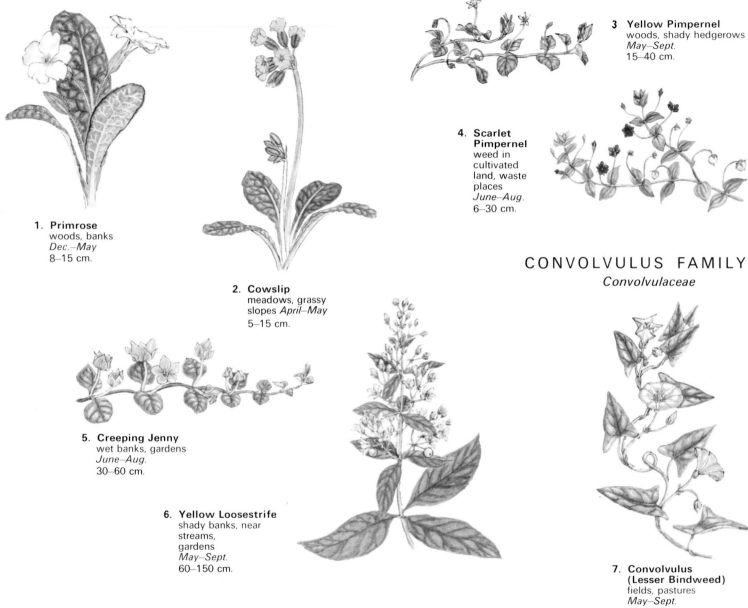

1. Primrose
woods, banks
Dec.–May
8–15 cm.

2. Cowslip
meadows, grassy
slopes *April–May*
5–15 cm.

3 Yellow Pimpernel
woods, shady hedgerows
May–Sept.
15–40 cm.

4. Scarlet Pimpernel
weed in cultivated land, waste places
June–Aug.
6–30 cm.

5. Creeping Jenny
wet banks, gardens
June–Aug.
30–60 cm.

6. Yellow Loosestrife
shady banks, near streams, gardens
May–Sept.
60–150 cm.

CONVOLVULUS FAMILY
Convolvulaceae

7. Convolvulus (Lesser Bindweed)
fields, pastures
May–Sept.
20–75 cm.

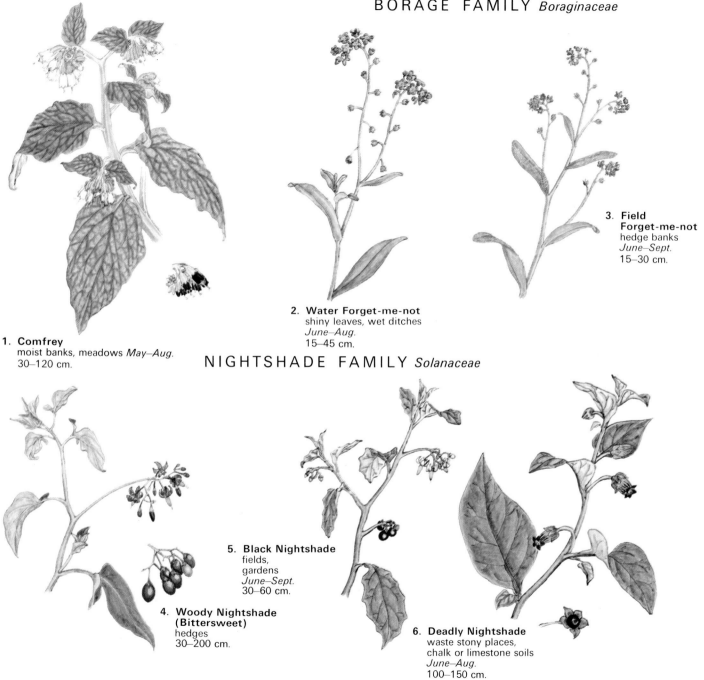

1. **Comfrey**
moist banks, meadows *May–Aug.*
30–120 cm.

2. **Water Forget-me-not**
shiny leaves, wet ditches
June–Aug.
15–45 cm.

3. **Field
Forget-me-not**
hedge banks
June–Sept.
15–30 cm.

NIGHTSHADE FAMILY *Solanaceae*

4. **Woody Nightshade
(Bittersweet)**
hedges
30–200 cm.

5. **Black Nightshade**
fields,
gardens
June–Sept.
30–60 cm.

6. **Deadly Nightshade**
waste stony places,
chalk or limestone soils
June–Aug.
100–150 cm.

FOXGLOVE FAMILY *Scrophulariaceae*
If the flowers are almost flat, it may be

1. Germander Speedwell
woods, grassland, hedgerows
May–Aug.
20–40 cm.

2.. Common Speedwell
woods, dry grassland
June–Aug.
10–40 cm.

3. Brooklime
wet ditches, streams
June–Aug.
20–60 cm.

6. Great Mullein
roadsides,
waste places
July–Aug.
20–300 cm.

4. Thyme-leaved Speedwell
field, waste places
June–Aug.
10–30 cm.

5. Buxbaum's Speedwell
cultivated fields, gardens
Jan.–Dec.
10–40 cm.

FOXGLOVE FAMILY *Scrophulariaceae*

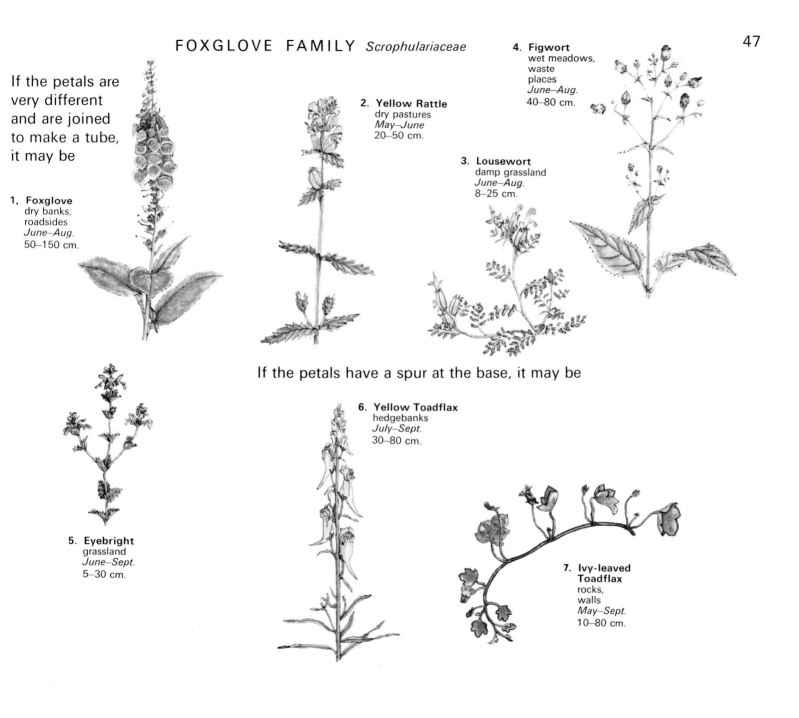

If the petals are
very different
and are joined
to make a tube,
it may be

1. Foxglove
dry banks,
roadsides
June–Aug.
50–150 cm.

2. Yellow Rattle
dry pastures
May–June
20–50 cm.

3. Lousewort
damp grassland
June–Aug.
8–25 cm.

4. Figwort
wet meadows,
waste
places
June–Aug.
40–80 cm.

If the petals have a spur at the base, it may be

5. Eyebright
grassland
June–Sept.
5–30 cm.

6. Yellow Toadflax
hedgebanks
July–Sept.
30–80 cm.

7. Ivy-leaved Toadflax
rocks,
walls
May–Sept.
10–80 cm.

If the top petals form a hood and the leaves are strongly scented when squeezed, it may be

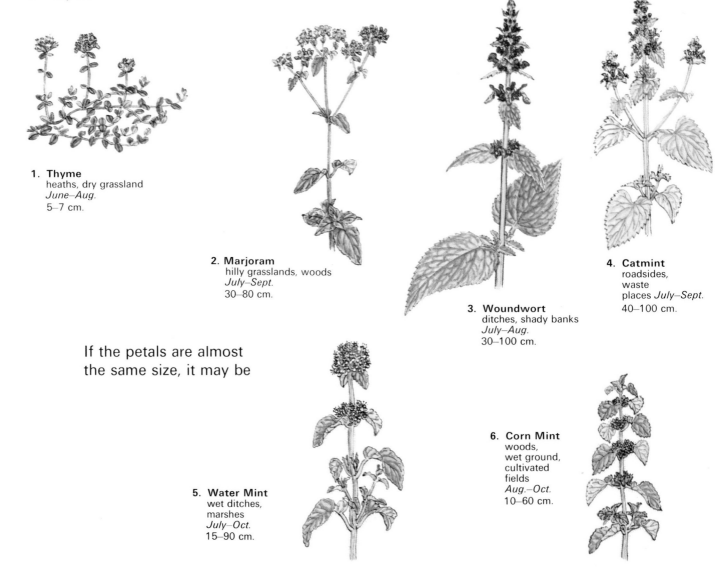

1. Thyme
heaths, dry grassland
June–Aug.
5–7 cm.

2. Marjoram
hilly grasslands, woods
July–Sept.
30–80 cm.

3. Woundwort
ditches, shady banks
July–Aug.
30–100 cm.

4. Catmint
roadsides,
waste
places *July–Sept.*
40–100 cm.

If the petals are almost
the same size, it may be

5. Water Mint
wet ditches,
marshes
July–Oct.
15–90 cm.

6. Corn Mint
woods,
wet ground,
cultivated
fields
Aug.–Oct.
10–60 cm.

If the top petals form a hood and the leaves are **not** strongly scented, it may be

Red Deadnettle
garden weed,
waste places
March–Oct.
10–45 cm.

2. Ground Ivy
hedges, woods,
waste places
March–May
10–30 cm.

3. White Deadnettle
banks, waste places
May–Dec.
20–60 cm.

4. Hemp Nettle
fields, waste places
June–Aug.
10–100 cm.

If the flowers
have very small
upper petals,
it may be

7. Bugle
damp woods,
meadows
May–July
10–30 cm.

Self-heal
banks, grassland
June–Sept.
5–30 cm.

6. Betony
open woods, hedgebanks,
grassland, heaths
June–Sept.
15–60 cm.

DAISY FAMILY *Compositae*

If the florets are all cup-shaped (page 4) and the fruits have a long pappus (page 13) it may be

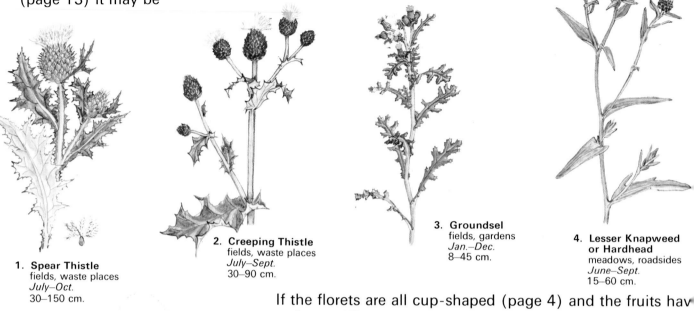

1. Spear Thistle
fields, waste places
July–Oct.
30–150 cm.

2. Creeping Thistle
fields, waste places
July–Sept.
30–90 cm.

3. Groundsel
fields, gardens
Jan.–Dec.
8–45 cm.

**4. Lesser Knapweed
or Hardhead**
meadows, roadsides
June–Sept.
15–60 cm.

If the florets are all cup-shaped (page 4) and the fruits have a short, stiff pappus (page 13) it may be

5. Coltsfoot
(flowers appear before the leaves)
roadsides, waste places
Feb.–April
5–15 cm.

6. Greater Knapweed
dry meadows, roadsides
July–Sept.
30–90 cm.

7. Burdock
roadsides, waste places
June–Aug.
60–120 cm.

If all the florets are strap-shaped (page 4)
and yellow, and the pappus (page 13) has
simple hairs it may be

1. Dandelion
   meadows, waste places
   March–Oct.
   5–20 cm.

2. Smooth Hawk's-beard
   dry banks, waste places
   June–Sept.
   20–90 cm.

3. Common Hawkweed
   banks, woods, meadows
   July–Aug.
   20–80 cm.

If the florets are all cup-shaped (page 4),
but the fruit has no pappus (page 13)
it may be

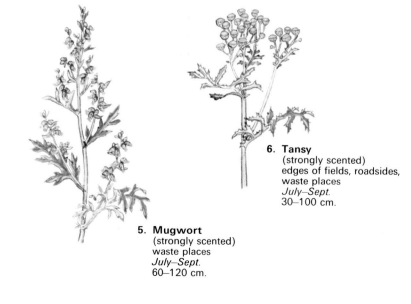

4. Sow Thistle
   (stem has a milky juice)
   fields, waste places
   June–Aug.
   20–150 cm.

5. Mugwort
   (strongly scented)
   waste places
   July–Sept.
   60–120 cm.

6. Tansy
   (strongly scented)
   edges of fields, roadsides, waste places
   July–Sept.
   30–100 cm.

If all the florets are strap-shaped (page 4) and yellow, and the pappus (page 13) is feathery it may be

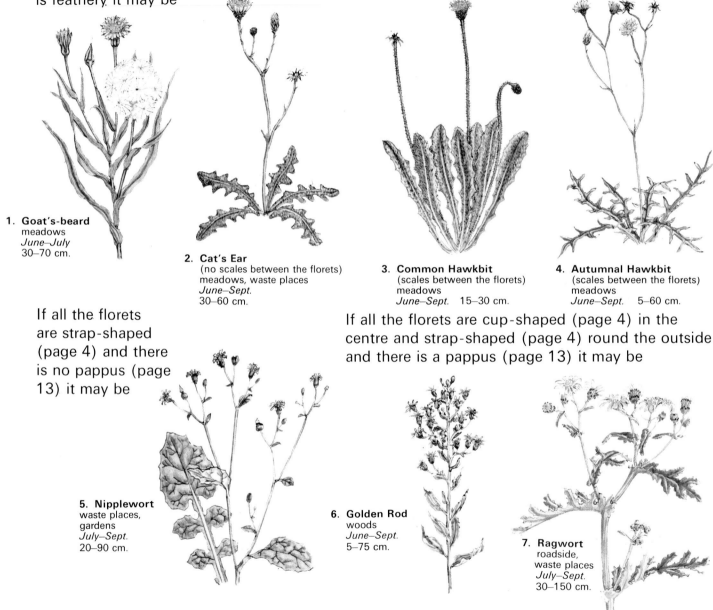

1. Goat's-beard
meadows
June–July
30–70 cm.

2. Cat's Ear
(no scales between the florets)
meadows, waste places
June–Sept.
30–60 cm.

3. Common Hawkbit
(scales between the florets)
meadows
June–Sept.   15–30 cm.

4. Autumnal Hawkbit
(scales between the florets)
meadows
June–Sept.   5–60 cm.

If all the florets are strap-shaped (page 4) and there is no pappus (page 13) it may be

If all the florets are cup-shaped (page 4) in the centre and strap-shaped (page 4) round the outside and there is a pappus (page 13) it may be

5. Nipplewort
waste places,
gardens
July–Sept.
20–90 cm.

6. Golden Rod
woods
June–Sept.
5–75 cm.

7. Ragwort
roadside,
waste places
July–Sept.
30–150 cm.

If the florets are cup-shaped (page 4) in the centre, strap-shaped (page 4) round the outside and have no pappus (page 13) it may be

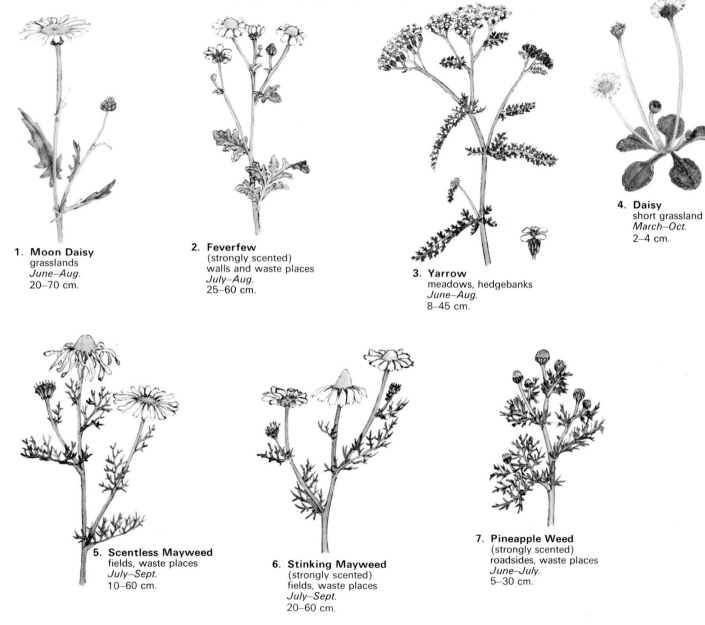

1. **Moon Daisy**
grasslands
June–Aug.
20–70 cm.

2. **Feverfew**
(strongly scented)
walls and waste places
July–Aug.
25–60 cm.

3. **Yarrow**
meadows, hedgebanks
June–Aug.
8–45 cm.

4. **Daisy**
short grassland
March–Oct.
2–4 cm.

5. **Scentless Mayweed**
fields, waste places
July–Sept.
10–60 cm.

6. **Stinking Mayweed**
(strongly scented)
fields, waste places
July–Sept.
20–60 cm.

7. **Pineapple Weed**
(strongly scented)
roadsides, waste places
June–July.
5–30 cm.

SCABIOUS FAMILY *Dipsacaceae*

BELLFLOWER FAMILY *Campanulaceae*

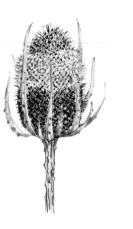

1. Field Scabious
woods, grasslands,
hedgerows
July–Sept.
25–100 cm.

2. Teasel
roadsides, waste
places
July–Aug.
50–200 cm.

3. Harebell
hilly grasslands
July–Sept.
15–40 cm.

4. Nettle-leaved Bellflower
hedgebanks, woods
July–Aug.
50–100 cm.

BEDSTRAW FAMILY *Rubiaceae*

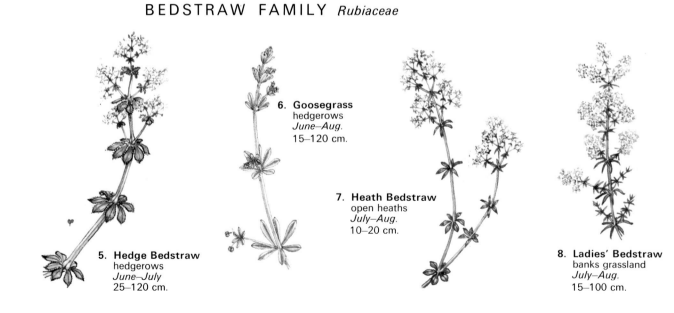

6. Goosegrass
hedgerows
June–Aug.
15–120 cm.

7. Heath Bedstraw
open heaths
July–Aug.
10–20 cm.

5. Hedge Bedstraw
hedgerows
June–July
25–120 cm.

8. Ladies' Bedstraw
banks grassland
July–Aug.
15–100 cm.

PONDWEED FAMILY *Potamogetonaceae*

All pondweeds grow in water and have very long stems

1. **Broad Pondweed**
lakes, ponds, streams
May–Sept.

2. **Curled Pondweed**
lakes, ponds, streams
May–Oct.

3. **Opposite Pondweed**
shallow pools, ditches
May–Sept.

4. **Canadian Pondweed**
(*Hydrocharidaceae*)
lakes, ponds, streams
May–Oct.

DUCKWEED FAMILY *Lemnaceae*
These plants float freely on water;
flowers not often seen

5. **Lesser Duckweed**
ponds
June–July
1·5–4 mm across

6. **Ivy Leaved
Duckweed**
ponds
May–July
7–12 mm across

WATER PLANTAIN FAMILY *Alismataceae*

7. **Water Plantain**
watery ditches,
edges of streams
June–Aug.
20–100 cm.

LILY FAMILY *Liliaceae*

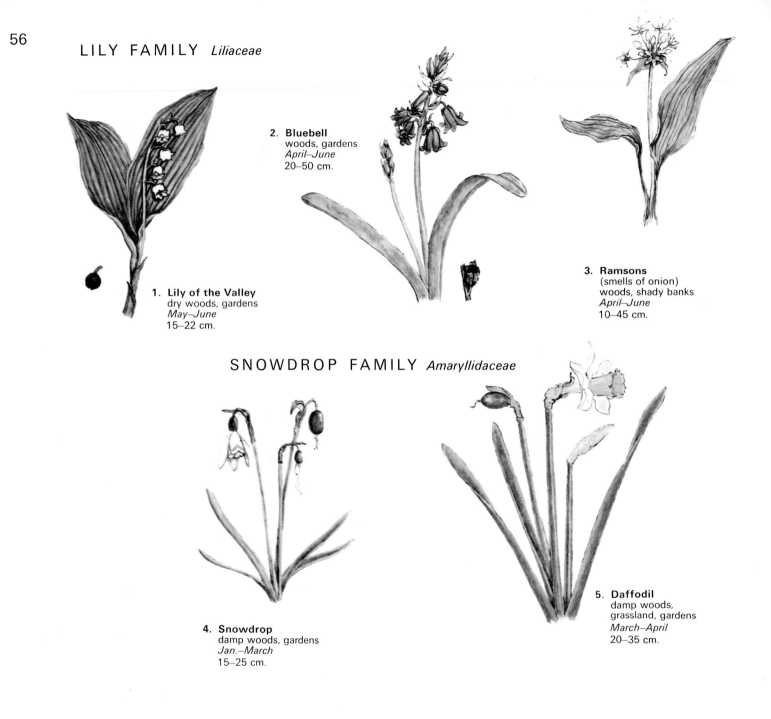

2. Bluebell
woods, gardens
April–June
20–50 cm.

1. Lily of the Valley
dry woods, gardens
May–June
15–22 cm.

3. Ramsons
(smells of onion)
woods, shady banks
April–June
10–45 cm.

SNOWDROP FAMILY *Amaryllidaceae*

4. Snowdrop
damp woods, gardens
Jan.–March
15–25 cm.

5. Daffodil
damp woods,
grassland, gardens
March–April
20–35 cm.

RUSH FAMILY *Juncaceae*

If the plant has long round leaves it may be

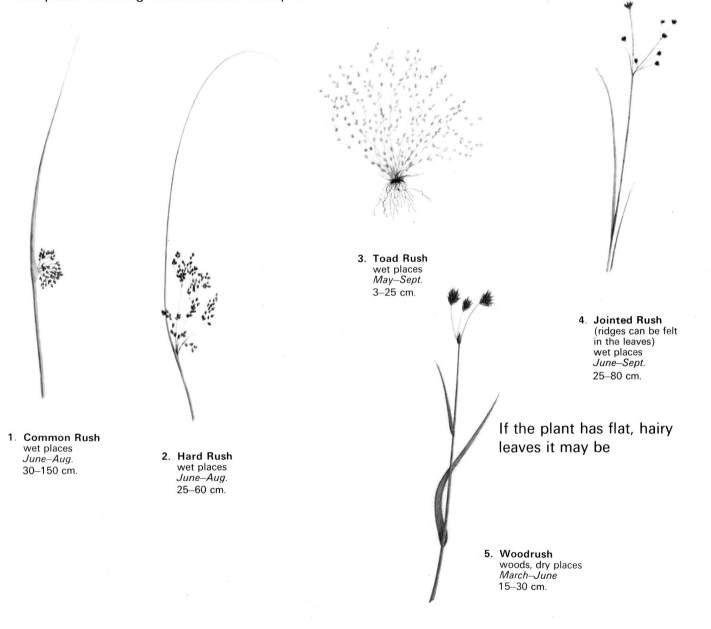

1. Common Rush
wet places
June–Aug.
30–150 cm.

2. Hard Rush
wet places
June–Aug.
25–60 cm.

3. Toad Rush
wet places
May–Sept.
3–25 cm.

4. Jointed Rush
(ridges can be felt
in the leaves)
wet places
June–Sept.
25–80 cm.

If the plant has flat, hairy
leaves it may be

5. Woodrush
woods, dry places
March–June
15–30 cm.

ORCHID FAMILY *Orchidaceae*

If the flower has a short spur (page 25) it may be

If the flower has a long, slender spur (page 25) it may be

If the flower has large lower petals that look like an insect's body it may be

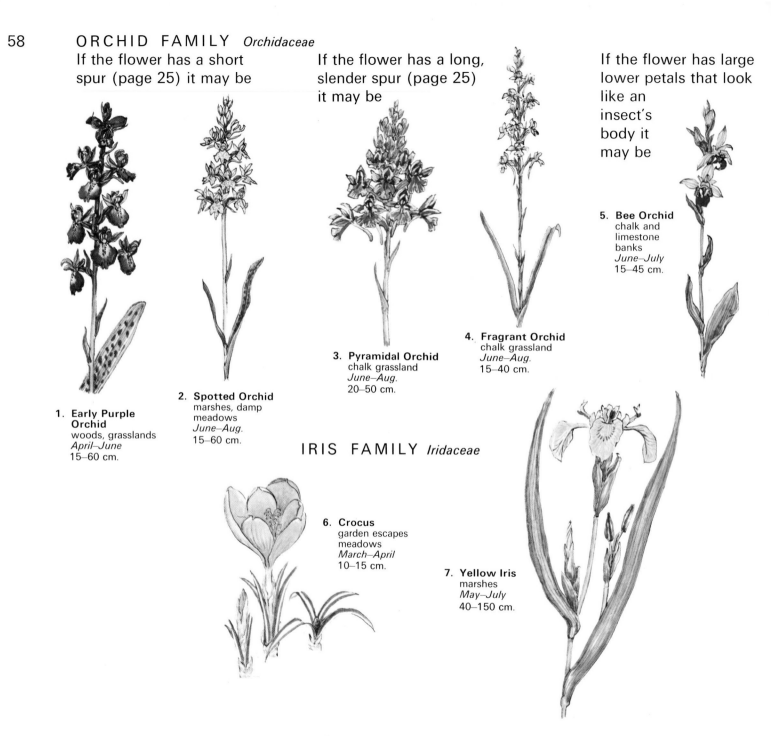

5. **Bee Orchid**
chalk and limestone banks
June–July
15–45 cm.

1. **Early Purple Orchid**
woods, grasslands
April–June
15–60 cm.

2. **Spotted Orchid**
marshes, damp meadows
June–Aug.
15–60 cm.

3. **Pyramidal Orchid**
chalk grassland
June–Aug.
20–50 cm.

4. **Fragrant Orchid**
chalk grassland
June–Aug.
15–40 cm.

IRIS FAMILY *Iridaceae*

6. **Crocus**
garden escapes meadows
March–April
10–15 cm.

7. **Yellow Iris**
marshes
May–July
40–150 cm.

If the stamens and ovaries (page 10) are in separate flowers in the same cluster it may be

If the stamens and ovaries are in separate clusters of flowers it may be

If the plant is like this it is

1. **Common Bulrush**
lakes, ponds, wet ditches
June–Aug.
100–300 cm.

2. **Common Sedge**
marshes, wet grassland
May–Aug.
7–70 cm.

3. **Carnation Sedge**
damp places
May–June
10–40 cm.

4. **Reedmace**
(*Typhaceae*)
lakes, ponds wet ditches
June–Aug.
150–250 cm.

GRASS FAMILY *Gramineae*

If the flowers are arranged in tight spikes it may be

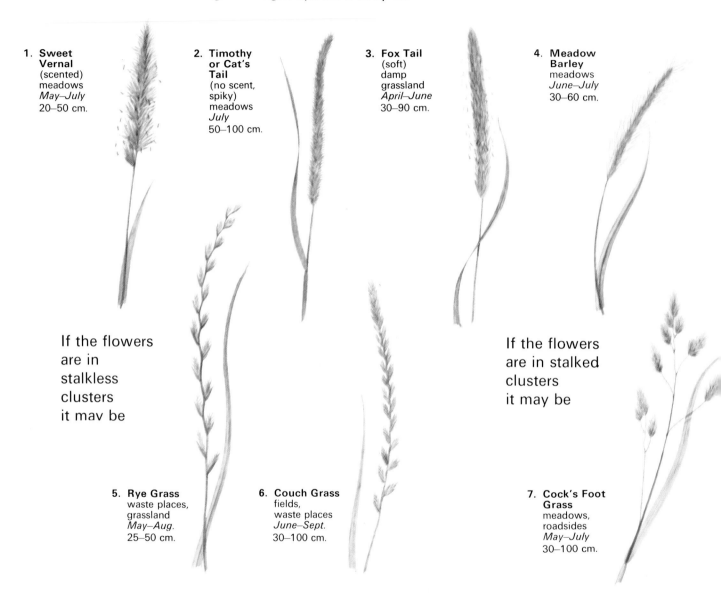

1. **Sweet Vernal**
(scented)
meadows
May–July
20–50 cm.

2. **Timothy or Cat's Tail**
(no scent, spiky)
meadows
July
50–100 cm.

3. **Fox Tail**
(soft)
damp
grassland
April–June
30–90 cm.

4. **Meadow Barley**
meadows
June–July
30–60 cm.

If the flowers
are in
stalkless
clusters
it may be

If the flowers
are in stalked
clusters
it may be

5. **Rye Grass**
waste places,
grassland
May–Aug.
25–50 cm.

6. **Couch Grass**
fields,
waste places
June–Sept.
30–100 cm.

7. **Cock's Foot Grass**
meadows,
roadsides
May–July
30–100 cm.

If the flowers have awns (page 10) and are in spreading clusters it may be

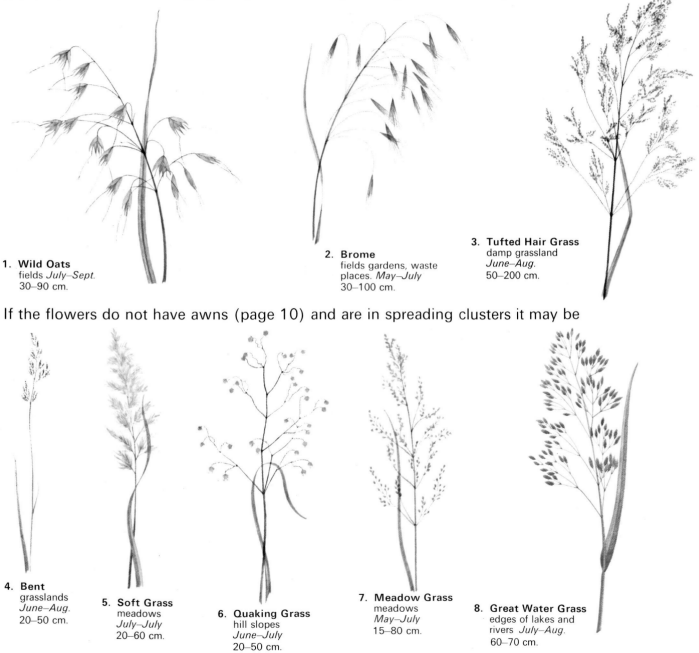

1. **Wild Oats**
   fields *July–Sept.*
   30–90 cm.

2. **Brome**
   fields gardens, waste
   places. *May–July*
   30–100 cm.

3. **Tufted Hair Grass**
   damp grassland
   June–Aug.
   50–200 cm.

If the flowers do not have awns (page 10) and are in spreading clusters it may be

4. **Bent**
   grasslands
   June–Aug.
   20–50 cm.

5. **Soft Grass**
   meadows
   July–July
   20–60 cm.

6. **Quaking Grass**
   hill slopes
   June–July
   20–50 cm.

7. **Meadow Grass**
   meadows
   May–July
   15–80 cm.

8. **Great Water Grass**
   edges of lakes and
   rivers *July–Aug.*
   60–70 cm.

Some WOODY plants; look in books about shrubs and trees for others

HEATHER FAMILY *Ericaceae*

1. Bell Heather
dry heaths
July–Sept.
60 cm.

2. Ling
heaths
July–Sept.
60 cm.

CONIFER FAMILY *Coniferae*

Pine
heathlands
May–June

Yew
hilly places
March–April

IVY FAMILY *Araliaceae*

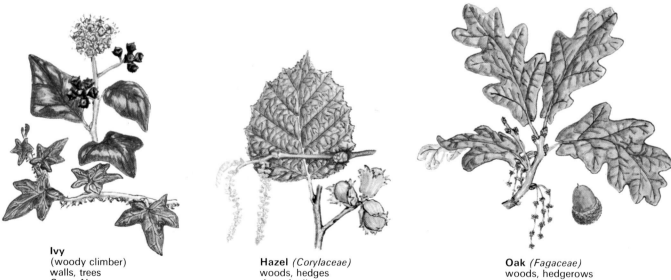

Ivy
(woody climber)
walls, trees
Sept.–Nov.

CATKIN FAMILY

Hazel *(Corylaceae)*
woods, hedges
Jan.–April

Oak *(Fagaceae)*
woods, hedgerows
April–May

Only the most common flowers in each family have been
illustrated in this book; if your flower is not illustrated look up
the family in another book.

Pocket Guide to Wild Flowers   D. McClintock and R. S. Fitter (Collins 1956)

Flowers of the Field   C. A. Johns (Routledge 1949)

Oxford Book of Wild Flowers   B. Nicholson, S. Ary and M. Gregory (O.U.P. 1960)

Concise British Flora in Colour   W. Keble Martin (Michael Joseph 1965)

Index